CHICKEN
SOUP
FOR
Betty
BOOP

A BOOK OF FUNKY POEMS
BY TOM CLEMENTS

Chicken Soup for Betty Boop

A Book of Funky Poems

Tom Clements

HIT 'EM UP PUBLISHING

346 Rheem Blvd, Suite 110-B
Moraga, California 94556
www.tctutoring.net

First Edition: January 2015

Cover and all interior artwork by NAMITA KAPOOR
www.namitakapoor.com

Printed in the United States of America

ISBN: 978-0-692-24019-9

For Michi

Preamble

What, I ask
Is poetry
Absent syncopated rhyme --
Kindred spirit to
Tequila, drunk
Sans salt
And lacking lime

SCIENCE

RELIGION AND PHILOSOPHY

WOMEN

SCIENCE

Pax Requiem

Like Icarus the Dodo bird did fly
Too far from home, too high
Above uncharted sea and like
That errant son his wayward hike
Panned out suboptimal, a poor solution
(At least in terms of evolution)
As the bird in flight at last alit
On the island of Mauritius a bit
Perplexed to find sufficient stores of food
A dearth of predators, a perfect anti-Darwin party mood
Time to chill and chew the fat
Forget the gene pool and all that
Who knew that several generations hence
Those stubby wings would fail to recompense
The bird in flight
In fact, the grounded aviator might
Reflect upon the social cost
Of all that forbear DNA now lost
And in reflection contemplate the news
That sailing ships with cooks and cats and rats and hungry crews
Were soon to make their way along the coast
And Dodo birds, pax requiem, would soon be evolutionary toast

Heat Death

Each day the world winds down
A little more, the second law
Outweighs the first
Heat flows, as Clausius would say
From hot to cold
Things move from bad to worse
The flaw not in ourselves
But in our stars
Which fund the flow
Together we grow weak and old
Until at last
The present and the future
Meet the past
And then all three are one
Lukewarm, indifferent and undone

Backstreet Boys

Servlets come and servlets go
Busy on the backend so
The browser gets a breather
Either that
Or drive the information superhighway
With a flat

Neoteny

Ontogeny recapitulates phylogeny
Just a fancy way to say
A hairy zygote in a Petri Dish
Begins life as a fish
Think that's odd, a little later
The embryo's an alligator
What comes next, a horse, a camel?
Pretty much, in any case a mammal
Takes the stage and we debate
The evolution of a tunicate

Conjugate Pairs

Put two acids in a pot
The weaker one, which knows its place
Becomes a base
The stronger one does not

If the base begins to fuss
Unhappy with its new H+
Reverse the order, clear the slate
It's now the acid conjugate

Neglecting Air Resistance

Drop two objects off the roof
As Galileo did, providing proof
That masses hardly matter
Skinny objects hit the ground
Neck and neck with fatter
The ratio of force to mass
Is fixed. The game's a draw
Inertia offsets gravity
Newton's second law

Trophlaxis

Ants do it as they scurry down the line
French kiss, that is
Swap spit
And bump and grind
The message is the medium
Trophlaxis, on the fly. They taste
Each other well beyond their haste
This interplay goes on all day
Until the colony at night
Exhausted from the constant kiss and tell
Puts out the light and dreams of being
Just a solitary cell

Wonder Bread

Fats don't make you fat
Unless entwined with carbohydrates
Sugar, alcohol, refined
And fabricated foods
Like Wonder Bread
And Frosted Flakes
Instead of pounds you lose
Your metabolic brakes
Can't stop, can't quit
Without your breakfast bagel
Pretty soon you're hardly able
To decamp, you sit
Strung out on starch
A one-time hot tomato
Wondering how you metamorphed
Into a couch potato

Quark Soup

Back at the beginning
Of the bang called big
When matter was at best
A single solitary mass at rest
Before the universe became diverse
Two elementary forces flew the coop
And for a fundamental moment we were all
Quark soup

RELIGION AND PHILOSOPHY

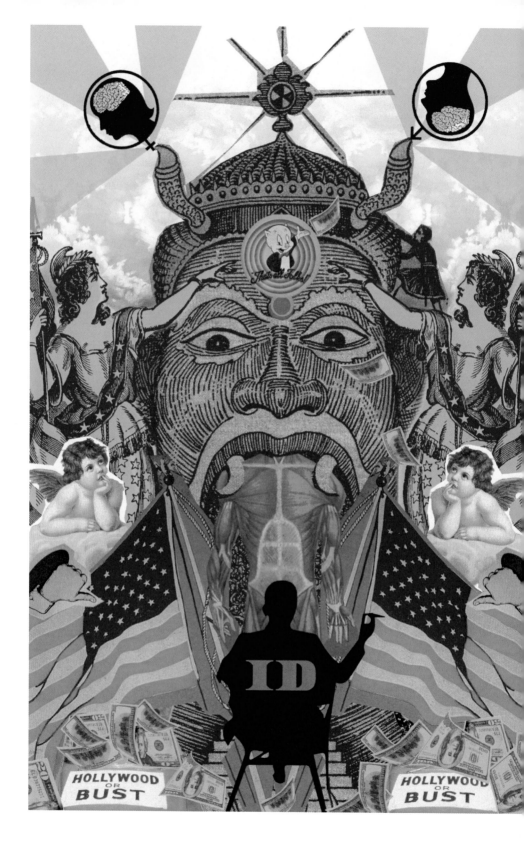

Best of Seven

Seven deadly sins to think on
Which one to call my own, at least
Enough to merit conversation
In the belly of the beast, not lust
Too many takers headed south toward
Hollywood or bust. Not sloth, I think
I'd sooner swim than sink
And envy, men from Mars, women Venus
Freud declared exclusive province
Of the penis. Wrath?
Don't make me laugh. Not greed
They say it tears a man to pieces
Striving to be rich as Croesus
Gluttony? -- whole hog -- a gig
More suited to the likes of Porky Pig

But pride, now there's a tried
And true, red white and blue
Diversion, worthy of a prince, in fact

Fallen angels, down from heaven
Recommend it as the very
Best of seven

From Bishop Berkeley's Point of View

If you were God
Before this galaxy got going
Before the world unfurled
And everywhere you looked
The look was you
No creature stirred, you hadn't yet
Proclaimed the Word
Much less inspired any Book
The only person at your party
Was you yourself. Not very cordial
Smarty. In fact a little creepy
When all around you
The only thought you get
In Latin yet, is:
Esse est percipi

Got Religion

When I was young and felt despair
I never made a fist and shook it
In the air. I never asked
The thunderstorm to quit
Or blamed the sun
Because the sky was poorly lit
I had no thought some god in heaven
Looking down would care
A tenant of the earth I had
A long-term lease and didn't need a Dad

Now I rant and rave and revel
Not alone but with my friend the devil
We take potshots
At the moon, curse the universe
And sleep till noon. Just two hotshots
Out to even up the score
Now, unlike before, I know this guy
Has something up his sleeve
But what the hell, I finally got religion
I believe

Extreme Unction

Fly in the ointment, oh poor fellow
Once so raucous, now so mellow
Out of body I observe
Your sticky torso, absent verve
Abnormally quiescent
Even still you seem to toil
Belly up in sacred oil

The priest makes tiny crosses
On my head. Ignores my severed leg
And spleen. Do I need confession?
Meter's running. Now come clean
A surrogate for Christ I think
He's out to cut his losses

And you, my languid metaphor for blunder
The priest has rubbed you in
Part and parcel of his antidote for sin
Now your mischief never ceases
As a dying amputee I wonder
Can't a fellow just be left
To die in pieces

Niche Market

Some poetry is hard to fathom
Other poetry just serves
To scratch an itch
This poetry right here
Has universal meaning
To the extent this universe
Is just another niche

Skyjack

D. B. Cooper though you strapped the loot
Around your body with the parachute
Your motive wasn't mainly economic
You viewed the action as a social tonic
To restore
Man's faith in nature and the great outdoors
Blase about your new net worth
You knew your plans would finally bring you
Down to earth

And you knew the plot was too subliminal
To be thought the work of a common criminal
Let's just say you played your part disguised
As a member of this civilized
Community
And acted with a natural impunity
Like some dark angel or redeemer
Of a race too long content
With misdemeanor

The Last Kamikaze Pilot

Hachimaki on his head the fledgling pilot sat
Seiza, staring down at paper cranes and planes all that
An origami dream of art and valor
Spread out on the tatami mat, a grim tableau
Something old, a sword, a gun
And something new, a photograph of Tojo
Taken all together now he worked
Himself into a state of hollow grace
His collage a kamikazi mojo, yes
He had it working. No dishonor, only death
At dawn he packs his toys, his orders come
Head east across the ocean for the rising sun

Zen

Buddhists aren't big
On churches, on mission
Their chapel of choice
The human condition
Not where they're going
Not where they've been
They dote on the moment
By factors of ten
Absent ambition, agenda and fare
Once they get where they're going
They're no longer there

Boardwalk Buddha

Betty Boop was not
Your average cartoon flapper
That miss-proportioned head
Those bee-stung lips
The sister
Had such rotation in her hips
No flatland romeo
Could long resist her

Her eyes
Black holes in space
Her mind
A coney island of the kind
That Ferlinghetti sought
Her legs all taut
Intentions randy
Watching her on screen was like
Consuming cotton candy

Now today instead we're stuck
With guys like Mickey Mouse and Donald Duck
Whatever happened to my Boardwalk Buddha
Siren of serenity, who knew
That basic instinct would become so rare
That someone so *all there*
So full of quirky self-expression
Would hardly last beyond the Great Depression

Quartet

	Start	Finish
1950s	God, Motherhood, and apple pie	Joe McCarthy, Catcher in the Rye
1960s	Rosa Parks, the grassy knoll	Sex, drugs and rock-n-roll
1970s	Sharon Tate	Watergate
1980s	Corporate culture, disco duck	AIDS and junk bonds, what the fuck?

WOMEN

Body Heat

Kathleen Turner sits there on the beach
No Carioca she but full of body heat
The Ipanema sky is not too high
Her grasp does not exceed her reach

She wonders what became of Ned
Her heart not for a moment racing
Not old, not dead, she sees him
As a panther in a cage, still pacing

Round and round he goes
In a rage at knowing what he knows
Round and round he goes
In a rage at knowing what he knows

Broads

Broads, in his time
Sinatra knew a few
Big chested, prime
Never young enough
To get yourself arrested
Tough, gum chewing tarts
Like Judy Exner doing Sam
And sometimes Jack
Women who could take it
Women who could leave it
Women who could give it back
In spades. In hearts
Grown up girls a little bit
Too fond of pearls
Gun molls on the make
The farthest thing from pals with Bing
And utterly at odds with stable, safe, suburban
Happy housewifes lacking smarts
Their Doris Day-like, Deanna Durbin
Pajama-packing counterparts

Fabulosity

Life in the fast lane, it appeals to me
But all that glitter, I can take or leave it
Some guy comes on with champagne, roses, sturgeon eggs
Then tries to put his hand between my legs. Oh, please!
I'm outta there. You best believe it

Take someone like Onassis, take his yacht
There's still a million reasons not
To swab the decks, to swoon and grovel
Just because we sail the seven seas
Doesn't mean we're trapped inside a Harold Robbin's novel

When I was young my mama
Used to turn the dull and commonplace to drama
All she had to do was waive a pinky
Suddenly the landscape changed from rinky-dinky
To Shangri-La, to Pericles

Forget she ever went down on her knees
Those men with sad expressions kept
Their hats on in the room. Even when she laughed
She wept. Instead of gloom, she called me
Fabulosity
She never missed "I Dream of Genie" on TV

Shop Talk

Guys in high school, guys in college
Get away with murder. To my knowledge
Not one of them has ever read a book
On sex. Too bad, I only wish they had
A class in school like shop

Instead of cars, they let their girlfriends drop
Their skirts. Then every guy could
Learn to spend more time beneath the hood

Perfect QWERTY

Words of love are hard to type
Seasoned letter writers first subtract the hype
The mush, the gloden glow
Cutting to the chase we know
Is easier in fiction, there the siloutte
Conceals more than the hero or the heroine
Reveals, both parties playing hard to get

While here, my dear, it's just
Like peeling onions to reveal the core
A herculean task where less is more
Coalescing love and lust, declaiming
On the keyboard what I'm aiming to express
A love sublime, no less than down and dirty
A schizophrenic view, conveyed in perfect QWERTY

A Woman's Place

Men
Back then
So rough and tumble
Strong silent types. Full of body
Language, chutzpah, guts
A Marlon Brando mumble
Was the Gettysberg address
No more, no less, but just enough
To keep a woman in her place
The putz
Was full of savage grace

Pas de Deux

Dance it seems is nothing more
Than locomotion on the floor
Bodies tight, extended, slack
Breath in, breath out
Release, contract
No big deal, as I was saying
Part time job --
How much they paying?

Money doesn't matter, dear
It's not an IPO, I fear
You miss the metaphor, the point
Is not the locomotion
But the way the dancers show
Their angst, their outrage
At a world disjoint
It's all so very existential, don't you know

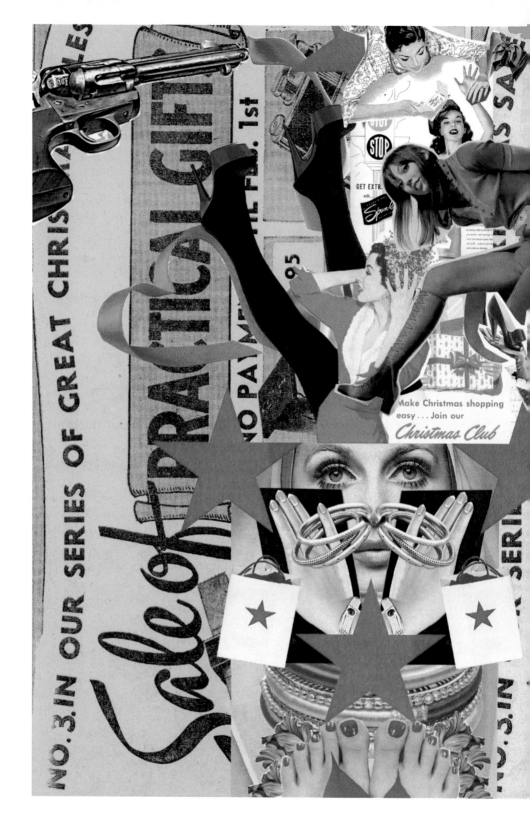

Spree

Macy's, Xmas shopping
Couple baby babes in platforms
Teeny bopping
Mop tops and tulip toes
Bangles, bracelets, earrings
Through the nose

On off, on off, off on
With lacies
Maybe one too many for the totebag
No one knows and yet
An aging, plain-clothes
Decoy jet-set vet

Behind a try-on curtain
Know's what's what
In no uncertain
Terms proclaims to one:
Forget it, cutie. That won't wash
While I'm on duty

Pulls out a gun, a badge, a belt
Cop props and then:

The old bag bags the bag
And busts the bebops
And then
The old bag bags the bag
And busts the bebops

Chicken Soup for Betty Boop

ABOUT THE AUTHOR

Tom Clements is an award-winning author of three test prep books teaching high school students how to write and analyze prose. He tutors SAT/ACT, physics, chemistry and calculus groups, helping kids get smarter AND get into college.

www.tctutoring.net